# Bug on the Beam

Cynthia Mercati
Illustrated by Freddie Levin

A Harcourt Achieve Imprint

www.Rigby.com
1-800-531-5015

Literacy by Design Leveled Readers: *Bug on the Beam*

ISBN-13:  978-1-4189-3664-8
ISBN-10:      1-4189-3664-2

Printed in China

3 4 5 6 7 8  985  14 13 12 11 10 09 08

Property of Rosa

# Monday, September 17

Dear Diary,

   This is the first time I'm writing because I just got this diary today for my birthday! My brother Carlos gave it to me and told me that I could use it to write down all of the things I am too shy to say.

   Carlos likes to tease me about being shy. He calls me Bug because I'm always hiding. I'm also really small for my age. I don't mind the nickname most of the time. Even though my real name is Rosa, everyone is starting to call me Bug!

# Wednesday, September 19

Dear Diary,

Today I did the bravest thing ever. Ms. Li, our P.E. teacher, is starting the school's first ever gymnastics class, and I signed up! Mom was very surprised when I told her because I am usually too embarrassed to do things like that in front of other people.

★New Gymnastics Club

★Meets every Tuesday and Thursday

★ Sign up sheet outside of the gym

But I really want to try gymnastics.

It all started when I watched the Olympics. The gymnasts all looked so calm and graceful. They seemed happy, and everyone in the audience clapped and cheered. If I could learn to move like them maybe everyone would stop calling me Bug!

# Thursday, September 20

Dear Diary,

　　We have so much to learn! Ms. Li made us stretch out every part of our bodies before we started class. If you don't warm up the right way, you can hurt yourself.

　　Next Ms. Li showed us the four pieces of equipment that girls use in gymnastics. There's the floor mat, the vault, the uneven bars, and the balance beam.

# Tuesday, September 25

Dear Diary,

I love gymnastics! I was thinking so hard today about what I was doing that I didn't have time to worry about anyone watching me.

When I did a handstand, I stayed up for six seconds, and all of the girls cheered. Then Olga smiled and said she could beat my time. (She did because Olga is best at everything.) I didn't mind because for the first time I felt as if I was part of a team.

# Thursday, September 27

Dear Diary,

Today Ms. Li showed us how to use the vault. First you take a fast running start and really pump your arms. You run toward the springboard and jump on it, and it pushes you into the air. Then you land on the vault with both hands. Since we're just learning, Ms. Li has to be there to help us flip and land on the mat.

The vault is really hard, especially because I'm small and not very fast. But for just a minute, when I was practicing the vault, I felt as if I was flying.

Mat

Vault

Springboard

# Tuesday, October 2

Dear Diary,

We moved on to the uneven bars today. First our class had to practice swinging on just one bar. Ms. Li said we should all walk on our hands from now on to develop our arm muscles. We all laughed and tried to picture walking through the hallways at school on our hands!

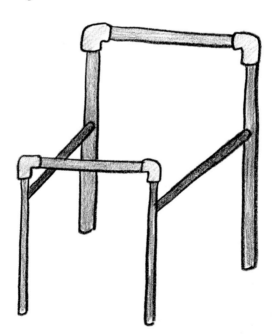

# Tuesday, October 9

Dear Diary,

I missed our last gymnastics class because I had promised to go and watch Carlos play baseball. So now I'm behind everyone else, and they're all better than me on the vault. I felt as if everyone was looking at me.

After class all of the other girls sat in the corner of the gym to eat snacks that their mothers had sent. At first I wanted to just go straight home because I still felt terrible about how I did in practice. But Olga sounded so nice when she asked me to sit down with them that I decided to stay.

I'm glad I stayed! Adele told me that she felt frustrated, too, when she had to miss practice a few weeks ago and that made me feel better. Also, her mom makes great blueberry muffins!

Me

# Thursday, October 18

Dear Diary,

Everything was going great until today. I've made new friends, and for the first time I feel as if I don't have to be embarrassed around other people. But today we started learning the balance beam, and I'm terrible at it!

The beam is four feet off the ground. (That's taller than I am!) Worse still, it's only four-and-a-half inches wide! I was all wobbly and scared just standing beside it! Then I got on and was even more wobbly. I nearly fell flat on my face.

# Saturday, October 20

Dear Diary,

I just had the worst nightmare of my life. I dreamed I was at gymnastics practice, and I was trying to stay on the beam, but I kept falling off. Finally I just wrapped my arms and legs around it, like it was a big tree trunk. All the other girls were looking at me and laughing. Olga kept saying, "Look at that little bug on the beam. She'll never make it across. She'll get squashed!"

## Tuesday, October 23

Dear Diary,

I have to face it. I'm hopeless! All the other girls are learning different tricks on the beam, and I can't even manage to stand up straight! No matter what I do, I always fall off!

All of the other girls look like
beautiful swans, and I feel like the
ugly duckling. Or maybe I should say,
they look like beautiful butterflies,
and I feel like the funny, little bug!
I wonder if I'll ever be able to do
anything with the balance beam
except fall off it.

# Thursday, October 25

Dear Diary,

Today Ms. Li said she was going to work with me on the basics of the beam again. I was a little embarrassed, but I really want to get better on the beam. First Ms. Li drew a box on the floor measuring the length and width of the beam. I walked forward and backward along it. I can do great on a flat floor!

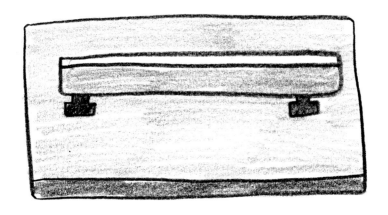

Next I moved on to the low practice beam, which is only a few inches off of the ground. I got to the end of the beam OK and then Ms. Li told me I had to walk backward!

My heart was pounding. I felt myself wobble, but I managed to get my balance. When I reached the other end without falling off, I couldn't believe it! Maybe I can learn how to walk on the beam after all.

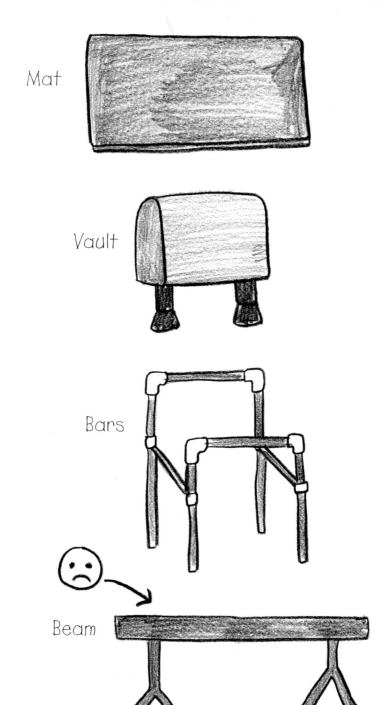

Mat

Vault

Bars

Beam

24

# Tuesday, October 30

Dear Diary,

I don't know whether to be excited or scared. Ms. Li told us today that she has entered us in a gymnastics meet on Saturday. I'm on a team with Adele, Olga, Emilia, and Tracy. We each have to perform on the floor mat, the vault, the bars, and (oh, no!) the beam.

I want to show my family what I've learned, but I'm afraid that I'll mess up! Ms. Li said that winning isn't important and we should all just have fun. That made me feel a little better, but I'm still going to practice hard to make sure I'm ready.

## Saturday, November 3

Dear Diary,

You won't believe what happened. At first everything was fine. My whole family came to my meet, and they all cheered for me from the stands.

Then it was my turn to walk on the balance beam.

I did everything that Ms. Li and I had worked on together. I didn't want to mess up and keep my team from winning. I bent down until I was sitting on the beam with my hands behind my hips to support myself. Then I lifted both legs up into a V position. I was doing it!

That's when it happened. My body started wobbling, and I knew I would fall off. I wrapped my arms around the beam and tried hard to stay on. I felt as if I was trapped in my own nightmare and I was going to get squashed!

I heard Olga and the other girls call out for me to be careful.

But it was too late. I fell off on to the mat below . . . splat! Just like a bug on a windshield!

I picked myself up and ran out of the gym trying hard not to cry. The thing I was most afraid of in the world—people looking at me and laughing—had come true. I pulled on my sweater, wondering why I'd ever thought that I could be a gymnast.

Carlos came to find me, and I told him I was quitting gymnastics.

He gave me a hug and told me that he would have missed out on a lot of fun if he had quit playing baseball the first time he messed up.

I asked him if it bothered him to mess up in front of other people. He said that it used to, but then he realized that everyone makes mistakes. It's important to keep trying.

## Tuesday, November 6

Dear Diary,

    I thought about what Carlos said. At practice today, I apologized to Ms. Li for running away and asked for a second chance. And she said that I could come back because the team needed me! All of the girls were happy to see me back on the team.

# Saturday, November 10

Dear Diary,

I'll probably never be very good on the beam, but everyone has different skills. Now I'm really good on the vault. And yesterday, Olga told me that my enthusiasm for gymnastics makes everyone happy! That's an important skill, too. I may never be a perfect gymnast, but right now I'm happy just being plain Bug!